COLORING OUTSIDE THE LINES

BY PHIL "RULE BREAKER" BOWYER

COPYRIGHT 2014

PUBLISHED BY
PHIL BOWYER & LIKEPHATE PUBLISHING
IN COOPERATION WITH PHIBBLE BOOKS

Dedicated to my beautiful wife Kate, who without her guidance, encouragement and a kick in the ass when I needed it, this book wouldn't have been possible.

Thank you my dear for your love, inspiration and wisdom.
I Love You.

Table of Contents

Introduction
Do You Have What It Takes To Color Outside The Lines?

Part I – Passion
Chapter One: Passion Trumps All
Chapter Two: Living Your Passion

Part II – The Brutal Truth: What Would You Say You Do Here?
Chapter Three: Who Are You? Really, Who The Hell Are You?
Chapter Four: Oh God It Hurts!

Part III – The Brutal Truth: How Bad Do You Want It?
Chapter Five: Get Out From Under The Covers
Chapter Six: Making The Lizard Brain Your Bitch
Chapter Seven: Quit Stalling And Make It Happen

Part IV – Getting Shit Done
Chapter Eight: Busy Versus Productive
Chapter Nine: You Can't Do It Alone
Chapter Ten: How The Hell Do I Do That Again?

Part V – Moving The Needle
Chapter Eleven: Failing Failure That Fails
Chapter Twelve: Are You Successful? Would You Know It If You Were?

Introduction
Do You Have What It Takes To Color Outside The Lines?

I was never one for coloring books. They seemed so restrictive. All those lines telling me where the crayon can and can't go. Oh, and don't get me started on the whole color by numbers thing. What's that about?

Even then I had to break rules by drawing my own pictures. I had to write my own rule book.

Over the years, breaking rules (or coloring outside the lines) has become my passion. My day is not successful unless I find a way to break at least one rule.

My rule breaking makes some people uneasy. Uneasy because I'm breaking the status quo and taking away their easy button. Uneasy because taking away the easy button forces them to embrace risk and leave their comfort zone.

For others, rule breaking inspires forward motion – true forward motion, not one based on danger numbers like follower counts or how many likes or shares your social media posts get.
The kind of forward motion which allows you to moves you closer, and closer to your Destination.

So what does breaking rules mean?

In 1984 I began what would be a ten year journey most boys dream about. I became a volunteer fireman for a small town outside of Chicago. Firefighters are extraordinary people. They run into situation others run from, literally. Firefighters intentionally put themselves into harms way to save lives and property.

The job is not what is extraordinary about my story. What is extraordinary is I was only fourteen years old at the time, a freshman in high school. I was the youngest member of our tiny two-station department which served slightly under 4000 people.

When my family moved to California in 1985, a fifteen year old did not have a chance being a fireman. I could have let this rule stop me, but that was not going to happen. The thrill of helping save a life and the rush of speeding to an emergency with the siren wailing and lights flashing was in my blood. I asked around and learned of the next best thing; the fire explorer program. This allowed me to continue my firefighting education and move closer to becoming a firefighter once again.

This experience was invaluable to me. I had the opportunity to lead an entire battalion in the Fire Explorer Academy, which were held at Camp Pendleton Marine Base north of San Diego California. This seven day academy not only kicked my ass, it taught me many things which I use to this day.

In 1988, less than a month after my high school graduation,

and about 3 months after my 18th birthday, I was hired as a firefighter for the Orange County Fire Department, where I stayed until I was bitten by the entrepreneurial bug.

I didn't realize it then, but my success in the fire service came from breaking rules. When my friends were out playing baseball, I was riding Code-3 to an emergency, or I was at the station learning my craft. I saw and did things most kids my age should not see or do, but I have no regrets, not even close.

In fact, it was probably the best thing I could have done. It's interesting that a paramilitary organization, which is all about falling in line and rules, would create the rule breaking monster you see before you today.

I learned while there may be rules of engagement in the fire service, they are nothing more than guidelines. Training is a big part of the job because we need to be extraordinary every time the alarm goes off. Being extraordinary means knowing each situation is unique and the rule book may not cover the situation you currently find yourself in.

In the fire service, we train using scenarios that help us see the big picture. You cannot foresee every situation, so being able to see and connect the dots is critical.

A business is much like an emergency call. Each one is unique and requires unique thinking.

As an entrepreneur you have rule breaking blood in you.

You have decided to go against the idea of getting a job working for someone else. Your business or idea breaks the status quo either by solving a problem that has not been solved or changing the way something is done.

It's in you. You are a rule breaker.

Breaking rules means you give up the easy button. Breaking rules means you stop applying other people's rules to your business. **Breaking rules means you write your own Rule Book.**

Following "top 10 things to do to drive traffic to your website" or "5 things successful people do every morning" will move you away from success. These things only work for the people who wrote them, not for the people who follow them.

I want you to stop and ask yourself the following question:

How will I stand out using cookie cutter advice that everybody else is using?

Could you answer it? No? Good.

The sad reality is entrepreneurs have become complacent and lazy. Sure, they work hard, but they work hard on *following*. Rule Breaking is about leading, but you cannot lead if you are following. This is why it is important to understand what your Destination is and to create your own map on how to get there.

The rules you hear experts talking about helped them reach their Destination. They were unique to them, and they worked beautifully. But, their Destination is not your Destination. They have no way of knowing where you are headed, so how can they possibly create a top ten list to guide you there?

Leaders ask the hard questions, and do the hard things to make forward progress. Leaders make their own decisions, and map out strategies to reach their goals. Leaders write their own rule book, and they *color outside the lines*.

"Our goals can only be reached through a vehicle of a plan, in which we must fervently believe, and upon which we must vigorously act. There is no other route to success."
-Pablo Picasso

What To Expect From Coloring Outside The Lines

This book isn't the kind of book you sit down and read. It is a hybrid between your traditional business book and a workbook. Each chapter has exercises which help you execute what you learned. Too many books throw stuff at you, and rarely is that information executed immediately, if at all. I am not going to give you an easy button (all the answers). These answers need to come from you and this book will guide you through the process of getting the right answers. They are right, because they are custom fit for you/your business, and you alone.

I also do not believe in writing a 327 page book, when 60 will get my point across. So, much like my first book, *Social Media Strategies*, this book is short, sweet and to the point. That said, don't think you can get through this book in a couple of hours (which you could if you only read it). If you follow all the exercises in the book, it will take you a couple of weeks or longer to complete. This may sound cliche', but the value is not in how many pages, but in the journey we will take within these pages.

Lastly, my personality is extremely evident in the following pages. As you read this book, you'll not only learn how to color outside the lines, but you will also get an insight into who I am, how I tick, and how I think, so consider that fair warning.

Before I Cut You Loose...

Grab a pen and some sort of notebook. I like the college ruled spiral notebooks (we load up on them during back to school month). Keep this handy as this will become your very own rule book to which you will color outside the lines.

Part One
Passion

"There is no passion to be found playing small – in settling for a life that is less than the one you are capable of living."

- Nelson Mandela

One

Passion Trumps Everything

Passion is any powerful emotion such as desire, love, hate and passion is the most important thing in our life.

The difference between work and play is passion. People get excited for the weekend because they can spend time on things they are passionate about instead of the mundane things they endure at their nine-to-five.

Passion for quality ingredients turns food into a collection of flavors, creating an explosion of pleasure that stays with you long after the meal. Passion turns chords and words into a powerful arrangement that calms the savage beast. Passion turns sex into wild, heart pounding, uninhibited lovemaking. Passion turns a junk yard relic into a beautifully restored muscle car capable of winning any street race.

Passion turns a boring life into a dream.

Passion isn't something you follow, because passion is not something to be pursued. Passion is something you live, breathe and experience every day. **Passion is the**

foundation for everything you do. Passion is your purpose.

TWO

Living Your Passion

Early on in our lives we choose a certain path. Maybe this path was not chosen, maybe we took it because it was expected of us. Maybe we did choose it, but found it was not what we thought it would be, but continued on anyway.

You may have thought because the first chapter was short, this book would be a breeze, but sorry, we are diving into the deep end!

Are You Living Your Passion?

Put the book down, and think about this. Really, do this and take your time. I'll be here when you are done.

What was your answer? Say it aloud. Do not simply mouth it, say it aloud. Make it tangible.

Now, to make sure your answer is true, and you are not bullshitting yourself, let's have a *Come To Jesus Meeting* – just you and me.

What is your passion? Write it down in your notebook.

"My Passion is _____."

Look at what you wrote. Study it.

Does it make you smile. Does reading those words make you want to put this book down and go work on it?

Looking back five days, have you worked on your passion? And, did that work put you in a good mood? Did your work excite you?

Would you still do it if you weren't getting paid (assuming of course your bills would be paid by the magical bill paying fairy)?

If you answered an emphatic "Yes" to all the questions above, skip forward to Chapter Three.

If you answered "No" to any or all of these questions – even if it's only one – then what you wrote down is likely not your passion. If what you are doing is causing you a great deal of stress – the kind that is overwhelming, or if working seems more like a chore, you my friend are in the wrong business.

But that is OK. We are going to fix it.

In your notebook, put a big X through what you wrote for your passion, and...

Turn the page. This is symbolic as it represents a fresh canvas for you to paint your future. You should feel excited right now at the possibilities that lie before you. Get pumped up, because by the end of this chapter you are going to want to celebrate (or at least split a Chimay with someone you love).

Discovering Your Passion

Remember those questions I asked earlier? Let's ask them a different way.

When you wake up in the morning, and slide out of the safety and warmth of the covers, what do you wish you were doing? What kinds of things do you like doing? What makes you smile? What are the things you cannot wait to work on?

And most simply, what makes you excited?

Pick up your notebook. You have a fresh clean page waiting for you to write down the answers to all of these questions. Put this book down, and spend some time with these questions. When you are done, I'll be here.

Take a look at what you have. Together, all of your answers make up your passion.

Turn the page in your notebook. Write down the answer to the following question:

What is your passion?

"My Passion is _____."

This time you should answer "Yes" to the following questions, if not, keep repeating this process until you do.

Look at what your wrote. Does it make you smile. Does reading those words make you want to put this book down and go work on it?

Looking back five days, have you worked on your passion? And, did that work put you in a good mood? Did your work excite you?

Would you still do it if you weren't getting paid (assuming of course your bills would be paid by the magical bill paying fairy)?

Part Two

The Brutal Truth What Would You Say You Do Here?

"Some people think that the truth can be hidden with a little cover-up and decoration. But as time goes by, what is true is revealed, and what is fake fades away."

- Ismail Haniyeh

THREE

Who Are You? No, Really, Who The Hell Are You?

One of the biggest fail points in business is neglecting to recognize and accept who we really are – the real person who lives down deep. This is a journey we never want to travel.

Discovering the real person can be a scary proposition, and while the road may indeed be filled with potholes and missing road signs, knowing the real you is the most important thing you can do.

It seems a right of passage to follow "successful entrepreneurs" and emulate them in every way we can. We subscribe to their newsletters, blog posts, YouTube – we absorb everything.

We become obsessed because we want their success. We want to be them. But, lest us not forget, we aren't them, and unless we have the exact same profile, following their checklists will get us as far as a car with no wheels.

Their *rules* worked for them is because their rules aligned with their personality, strengths and weaknesses. They are successful because they actually took the time to write their own rule book. If you want to truly be like them, then you need to write your own rule book too.

Writing your own rule book begins with understanding your personality, your strengths, and your weaknesses. In other words, your archetype.

Hey Look, A Squirrel

We live in a world where there is an abundance of distraction. We are so overwhelmed with choices to the point where ADD is commonplace. To make matters worse, everybody is competing for attention, using the exact same tactics.

Can You Handle The Truth?

Nobody gives a shit about your blog post, your video, or anything else. Why should they? You have not given them a reason to click your link. *What makes your link more special than the several hundred thousand other blog posts posted by entrepreneurs using the exact same tactic you are using?*

We have reached a point of immunity. We do not even see the "check out my blog" posts roll by anymore. The last thing we want to do is read some poorly written blog post by someone we do not even know, but somehow ended up connected to on the various social networks.

Buzzwords like "content marketing" have led everyone to create a blog, thus spamming the Internets with lame posts about "authenticity" when they themselves haven't a clue on what it means to be authentic because they have no clue who the hell they even are themselves.

This constant regurgitation of the same crap has created a culture of piggy backing on the hot topic of the day/week/month.

We ignore the crickets on not only our posts, but the posts of others who are doing the same thing. We even ignore our own behavior when confronted with these types of posts.

And then you have the others, you know who I am talking about. Posts by those influencers that people go nuts over. Their posts always seem to get the most shares and comments. What makes their post different?

Two things come into play here. First, they are doing it different, maybe offering a fresh approach to an old topic.

David Amerland talks about search, but he does not talk about SEO. He talks about how search engines work, and where search technology is heading, and how we can use this knowledge to our benefit.

His approach is quite different than the million SEO agencies writing blog posts on how rank #1 in Google ("Five

Things You Can Do Right Now To Rank #1 On Google"). This is why when David Amerland speaks, I listen. Not only does he know his shit, he's giving me something new to chew on and incorporate into my business strategies (notice I said *business* strategies, not Search Engine Optimization (SEO) strategies).

Next, we have archetype and personality. This is why we need to have a deep understanding of the *who* in our business. By understanding your *archetype*, you understand how the world sees you, which you use to communicate to your audience in a way that elicits the best response.

Personality is defined as an embodiment of qualities which we use to impress others. It is our character.

If we look to the psychological definition(3-1), it gives us a little more insight into what personality truly is;

(1) The sum total of the physical, mental, emotional and social characteristics of an individual.
(2) The organized pattern of behavioral characteristics of the individual.

It is no secret people buy from people, but it's not that simple. How is your personality affecting your ability to stand out and communicate? Are you using your natural archetype to your advantage, or working against it?

To answer these questions, you will need a deep

understanding of what makes you tick. We spend a lot of time analyzing others, but never ourselves.

Grab your notebook (and a shot of whiskey for courage) because it is time to learn all about your archetype. It's important to be brutally honest here. Do not bullshit yourself, and do not let anyone bullshit you either.

Turn to a fresh page and list all of your strengths, and on the next, write down all your weaknesses. I know, I know, but trust me, this is an important step because as we will talk about later, you won't be able to grow your business by yourself. By understanding your strengths and weaknesses, you will know how to build your team.

If you have not had that whisky shot yet, now would be a good time.

Once you have completed these two tasks, ask at least five people who know you well (friends and family – but not your mom.) to also list your strengths and weaknesses in your notebook. If you are on friendly terms with an ex, you might want to ask him or her to participate. Make sure they understand you want the brutal truth.

I am really sorry, but we are not done yet.

Find five more people (colleagues, acquaintances), and have them also write down their thoughts on how they see you.

Tell them to be brutally honest, and emphasize you won't hold what they say against them. People often tell us what we want to hear, so this is something you want to avoid (although I am sure your ex will have no problem with this).

I realize this could be a bit awkward, not only for you but for them, so it might be a good idea to do this over a beer. Better yet, do it over a meal.

Once you have collected your ten perceptions, come back and we will discover who you are.

Dissecting the information
I know asking friends, family and colleagues to rate you was extremely difficult and awkward. And, if you skipped it, shame on you.

Those pages in your notebook illustrate a picture of how your are perceived by the people around you. Take some time to compare how you think of yourself to how others think of you.

Do others think of you the same way you think of yourself?
What are the weaknesses others think you have, that you did not write on your list?
Identify strengths others wrote down, but you did not.
Are there any strengths on your list that are weaknesses on the lists of others?

I want to be clear, a weakness is not something bad, nor does it make you weak. The list of weaknesses you compile represents the things you should avoid because you are not good at them. Yes, the truth can hurt, but not as much as the lie.

One of the reasons Richard Branson succeeded where others failed was because he understood where his strengths ended and his weaknesses began.

Go Deeper
Psychology is fascinating to me, especially how it relates to marketing. I love to learn about how our mind works, specifically how triggers can make us do things under various circumstances.

In her book, *Fascinate*, Sally Hogshead illustrates seven triggers that captivate people. One of the perks of buying the book is the opportunity to get what Sally calls a "Fascination Advantage ® Report.(3-2) This report outlines the advantages that make up our archetype. This archetype is how the world sees you. While the goal is to be able to use this to communicate better with your audience, I also use it as a tool to look inside myself, so I can better understand who I am and what I offer my business.

FOUR

Oh God It Hurts

"*Oh, the pain, the pain.*" This famous phrase, uttered by Zachary Smith, anytime there was work to be done.

While some of you have no idea who Zachary Smith is (a fictional character from the *Lost In Space* television show), everybody has pain points. And pain is where we start putting the last few chapters to work.

Be Kind, Rewind
I think the definition of entrepreneur should be *someone who has a never ending stream of ideas*. The problem with ideas is they usually skip to the end. What I mean is you already know the *what*, but not the *why*. Instead of running forward with the idea, it is important to stop and go backwards. Yes, backwards. You need to reverse engineer the idea to get a deep understanding of what this idea exactly is, what it does, and who it serves.

There are three main parts of a product (in order of

importance):
(1) The Entrepreneur
(2) The Target Customer
(3) The Product Itself (The Idea)

I see many entrepreneurs fail because they developed the idea first, then hunted for the audience second. Many never factor themselves into the equation.

You, the entrepreneur, are the most important piece. Remember, passion trumps everything, and your passion for this product is what will make it stand out and make your audience take notice.

Ideas have a magical power. Let's be honest, we have a tendency to fall in love with our ideas pretty quickly. They seduce us, and make us do stupid things. But like any relationship, rushing to the bedroom, while wonderful at the time, eventually leads to a horrible, drama filled ending filled with regret.

You will be spending an extraordinary amount of time with your idea, and your relationship with it needs to be strong to endure the ups and downs the two of you will experience.

Infatuation or True Love?
It is hard to tell sometimes if an idea is simply something cool that somebody should do (infatuation), or something that will get you to your Destination (true love).

An idea based on physical attraction is not going to get you to where you want to go, so before anybody gets hurt, ask this simple question of yourself:

Is this idea aligned with my passion?

Remember, your passion trumps everything, and is the foundation for everything you do. It does not matter if this is a new idea, or an idea you have already executed. The sooner you know the answer to this question, the better chance you will have at success.

As your idea evolves, it is important to ask this question. *Is this idea still aligned with my passion?* The second the passion dies, so does the relationship with your idea.

The pain point

Steve Blank once said "no plan survives first contact with customers". What makes this statement so powerful is it gets the entrepreneur to think about the customer. It helps you create a plan that has already touched the customer, therefore having a better chance at success.

Special Note: This is where some rules come in which should never be broken. I am generally against checklists, formulas, or recipes, but like rules, there are exceptions. There are just some things that are what they are because human psychology is what it is.

Finding The Pain Point

A pain point (or often called friction point, or tension point) is something that causes pain to your target customer. It's called the pain point because your customer suffers from this particular problem. I had a pain point with my old oven. The broiler was in a drawer at the bottom. It was a pain in the ass to use because of it's location, and the fact that it was in a drawer. This pain point was solved by other manufacturers that put the broiler inside the oven, making it more accessible and easier to use (although I lost the ability to use the broiler and oven at the same time, an unintended benefit of the drawer style broilers).

As I joked earlier, there is no shortage of ideas in the mind of an entrepreneur. It is important to weed out the good ideas from the bad. Not all ideas solve a pain point, and not all ideas solve a big enough pain point to sustain a business.

When developing your ideas, do not be afraid to go a little crazy. This is your passion after all, and it should be fun. Ask disruptive "what-if" type questions that challenge assumed norms. Write down any and all ideas, no matter how wacky or impractical they seem.

Once you have your ideas, you can begin to narrow them down by asking if the idea aligns with your passion. If it does not, it gets cut, no exceptions.

Of the remaining ideas, ask the following questions:
What pain or tension point does my idea solve?
Who has this pain point?

How does your idea solve the pain or tension point?
Why does the person care about your solution?

All of these questions are focused on the customer, and their need, desire or want, not yours. While your business is about you and your passion, your product offering is about the people you choose to serve. Answering these questions keeps you focused on them, making your product more captivating and desirable.

Open your notebook.

Write down your idea.

OK, now go through the process outlined above, writing all the answers in your notebook. When you are done, ask the always important question:

Does this idea align with my passion?

If the answer is *yes*, then this is an idea worth developing further. If the answer is *no*, park the idea in a safe place to revisit at a later time.

Part Three
The Brutal Truth

How Bad Do You Want It?

"There are only two mistakes one can make along the road to truth; not going all the way, and not starting."
-Buddha

FIVE

Get Out From Under The Covers

Comfort is a special, yet controlling feeling. Our body kept warm and cozy, surrounded by soft sheets and blankets, while our head rests on the softest of pillows is like a little devil on our shoulder telling us to ignore the world and stay in bed all day.

A rough day probably includes "comfort food", which typically includes that of the junk food variety (did someone say Ben and Jerry's?).

The way an oversized chair hugs us makes us think twice about getting up to work on our passion, instead opting for another episode of *Californication*, or reading another chapter in our book.

Comfort feels good, but it can have an evil streak, especially when it comes to life as an entrepreneur. Yes, I'm talking about comfort zones. Comfort zones put us in a rut, and make us do things contrary to not only our overall personality, needs and wants, but also to our own reasoning. Comfort zones seem to have veto power over everything we want to do which has even the smallest element of risk involved.

The Amygdala, (More Commonly Known as the Lizard Brain)

The amygdala is a part of the temporal lobe in the brain, and part of the limbic system. The amygdala is responsible for the processing of memory, decision making, and emotional reactions. It's also responsible for creating the comfort zones that make us feel so safe.

Decision making and emotional reactions are like oil and water as opposed to the more favorable chocolate and peanut butter. When your mad or scared, you do not always come to the most logical decision. This is why, when you are all safe and warm under the covers, the idea of sitting at your desk working on something that could fail seems like a bad decision, preventing even the most excellent of ideas from being realized.

Size Matters

The larger the amygdala, the more anxiety we feel. This means, those who have a larger amygdala will have a stronger sense to stay in their comfort zone. It is much harder to say no to sitting in a comfy chair reading a good book while the rain pitter patters outside. It's not only the comfy chair scenario, it is also "playing it safe" when you actually do make it to your workspace.

What Is A Comfort Zone?

Simply defined, it is a rut which prevents you from taking your idea to it's fullest potential. If you do these things, you are probably suffering from *comfortzonitis*:

If you read a blog post instead of working on your idea, you might have *comfortzonitis*.
If you say things like, "I need to learn how to do this before I can work on...", you might have *comfortzonitis*.
If you censor or avoid being controversial in your idea in any way, you might have *comfortzonitis*.
If you spend a lot of time on email, social media or other distractions, you might have *comfortzonitis*.
If your behavior sabotages work on your idea, you my friend, have *comfortzonitis*.
If you are thinking like you did yesterday, you definitely have *comfortzonitis*.

Let me be clear, we all suffer from *comfortzonitis*. It is OK to be scared or unsure. It is natural, but we cannot let it paralyze us.

Embracing Risk Is The Antidote For C*omfortzonitis*

Entrepreneurship is about taking risks, trying new things, and being uncomfortable. It's the kind of uncomfortable which keeps you on the edge of your seat. Kind of like a scene in a scary movie when you are not quite sure what's around the corner but you cannot wait to find out. The kind of uncomfortable that grows you as a person. It is the kind of uncomfortable that feels good because you are breaking rules, and you aren't even thinking about apologizing for it!

If you fear something, it is something you should probably do (some call it "facing your fears" but I call it "flipping off your oversized amygdala").

Risk Takers Are Rewarded
Fighting your amygdala isn't always easy. In the next chapter I'll show you to make your lizard brain your bitch by modifying your habits and lifestyle, reducing it's hold on you, and make it easier to say no. No matter what we do to reduce it's influence over us, our lizard brain is a part of us, so it is important we learn how to say no.

Think Riskier
What is something you have never done before? It can be a trying a new dish, a change in your walking routine, drinking a beer in the middle of the day or even engage in some afternoon delight (don't laugh, it does wonders for energy and creativity). Do anything that shakes things up a bit.

Once you have got a taste of the good life, work business into it. Write a controversial blog post instead of sticking with the conservative route you have always taken*. Put a little more effort into Google+ or maybe you start writing the book you have been too scared to start on.

The whole point of taking these steps (starting out small, and working your way up) is to build your confidence and move you forward. The more confidence you have, the more success you'll have at your fingertips.

Open your notebook, and lets get real.

Write down three things you think you would/could never do. Leave some space in between each risky thing.

Next, under each one, write down why they are risky, and why you wouldn't do them. Are these things truly risky, or has your lizard brain blown them up into something larger than it actually is?

*By controversial I mean a post that expresses an opinion that you truly feel, but may be something that others do not agree with you, or like. Do not be afraid to express yourself, even if it may go against the grain. I am not advocating creating controversial posts only to get attention.

SIX

Making The Lizard Brain Your Bitch

As we just now learned, our lizard brain can be a controlling and manipulative pain in the ass that prevents us from living our passion.

The bad news is, it's a part of who we are, and will always be there to influence our decisions. The good news is, manipulation doesn't have to be a one way street. There are a few factors that can enhance the influence of our lizard brain; lack of sleep, sugar, lack of downtime/play and absence of routine. By reducing these factors, we have more control.

Sleep

Being an entrepreneur has it's challenges, not the least of which is sleep. We tend to take sleep for granted. "I'll sleep when I'm Dead" is a common joke response for those who work too much. The thing is, if you do not get your sleep you won't be doing anybody any good, most of all yourself.

Sleep is the best example of friends with benefits. Sleep is when the body repairs itself and becomes stronger. This is of course dependent on a number of factors like diet and the ability to enter a deep sleep (REM).

Remember the amygdala, or lizard brain, is responsible for memory, decision making and emotional reactions. Think about when you are tired, or someone you know who is tired. All three of these functions are inhibited and work against our best interest.

Memory
What was I saying? Oh, yeah. When you are tired, you have trouble remembering things. You forget where you left the keys, or why you are standing in the kitchen.

You also have trouble thinking on your feet. As an entrepreneur, we often need to have answers ready at will, and the inability to remember a simple fact (like a benefit of a product we invented) can be not only embarrassing, but damaging to our reputation.

Decision Making
The inability to make the right decisions can have a drastic impact on your business (like staying in a comfort zone). Lack of sleep causes lack of focus, which leads to poor decision making.

You know what I am talking about. When you are tired, your brain feels fuzzy, and unclear. Concentration is difficult to near impossible. You do your best to power through, but the reality is you are not working at your best – not by a long shot.

Your sense of reality is skewed, much like it is on alcohol or drugs. You know the scene in *Wolf Of Wall Street*, where he was so proud of himself for getting both his car and himself home without a scratch only to realize later he totaled his car, and created a path of damage? You may think you are making the right decisions, but the reality may be much different.

This lack of focus also has severe implications for your creativity. No matter what business you are in, creativity is a factor in reaching and sustaining success.

Emotional Reactions
When we are tired, we go through a wide range of emotions. For me, it starts out as "crabby". I'm a bear to be around because I snap at people and my already low patience drops to zero. I have no tolerance for anything.

As time progresses, I become less irritable as my wacky side comes out. I get funny and do not take anything too seriously. As you can tell from how this book is written, and the examples I use, I'm a pretty loose, funny dude, but the extreme version comes out when I am tired.

Whether we like it or not, emotions are very powerful and influence our actions. Emotions and business can mix, but only in the right amounts.

But Wait, There's More
Sleep does not only make our amygdala work better, but it also helps kill inflammation (the cause of most of our ailments, including that headache or stuffy nose), helps with

weight loss (in a world that judges on looks, looking good can do wonders for your business), and it gives us more energy (couldn't we all use that?).

How Many Hours Should You Get?
I get asked this one a lot. The answer is simple, but not easy. It is whatever your body tells you is enough. That could be 6 hours, or it could be 10. I average about 7, which is quite the difference from the 2 – 3 I was getting during the dreaded "insomnia years".

Sugar
Sugar is wonderful. It tastes delightful, and is comforting (I know I heard somebody say Ben and Jerry's this time). Simply looking at a beautifully decorated cake, or a golden brown cinnamon roll, or a slice of pie is enough to send our lust trigger into overdrive (and hopefully you won't find yourself drooling over your new shirt).

What I am about to say is not something you want to hear. Sugar is a toxin. It goes much deeper than making you fat. It messes with your entire system, including your amygdala.

Sugar is addictive (it's nearly impossible to say no to a piece of cheesecake). According to Dr. Cate Shanahan, sugar consumption releases brain chemicals called endogenous opiates. These chemicals make you feel so good, you do stupid things. (6-1)

Dr. Mercola adds sugar contributes to insulin and leptin resistance. Both of these play key roles in mental health.

He also points out, sugar inhibits BDNF (brain derived neurotrophic factor), a growth hormone responsible for promoting healthy brain neurons. Low levels of BDNF are commonly found in patients who are depressed.(6-2) Depression leads to a greater need for a comfort zone, and puts the "fight or flight" feature of your amygdala on overdrive.

Avoiding sugar is not easy. It's not only in the obvious places like soft drinks and sweets, but in all processed foods and alcohol. I would need a whole different book to answer the question on how to avoid the dangers of sugar, but there is a way to start small and have a big impact. Try avoiding soft drinks and other sweets (including that caramel macchiato) for one month and see how you feel. Yes, the cravings will be severe (which can be stayed off with some **high quality** dark chocolate (65% cocoa or higher).

Playtime & Downtime

Swings, monkey bars, slides and getting dizzy on the merry go round. Yeah, those were the days. We should all be more like kids, especially when it comes to playtime and downtime.

We live in an excessively hectic world. Technology is not confined to an office anymore, it follows us everywhere we go. The idea of being constantly connected to news, information, and the goings on of the people we care about, and the celebrities doing stupid shit, seems really cool, but the "always on" lifestyle takes its toll. We do not relax anymore because anytime our phone goes "ding", we pick it up to see what it's all about.

We have been told if we take a break we are lazy. We need to work harder – work, work, work, work, work! And then, work some more. That is utter nonsense. While it's true hard work begets success, over work is actually the enemy to success.

Go Play
Get the blood moving. Go to the park and act like a kid. Yes, people may look at you a little weird, but who cares – you are on a swing trying to touch the sky with your toes! Go for a walk and clear your head of stress and the bad mojo of the day. Meditation and yoga are also great ways for clearing the psyche of stress and bad stuff.

Take the love of your life to drinks and tapas. If you are the wiggling type, go dancing (and if you're not, the drinks may help).

Play fetch with your dog, gather some friends and play darts, or frisbee golf, go swimming, read a book (fiction), have sex, go shopping (you're welcome ladies), cook a nice meal – do something that doesn't involve your business or being in your work environment.

Do not wait until you need a break. Schedule it, make it part of your day. And that brings me to something which ties it all together – Routines.

Routines

If we look at a few artists who not only lived their dream, but found success, we notice the one commonality between them is routine.

> *"**Be regular and orderly in your life, so that you may be violent and original in your work."**
> -Gustave Flaubert*

We tend to avoid routine because it is boring and unexciting. We expect our day to be rich with excitement and adventure and routines kill the mood.

I think part of the problem with routines is they are typically built around society's need to make everything generic and one-size-fits-all. We have certain expectations of how our day should flow, including when we should eat our meals, sleep and work.

When we break away from society's rules, routines become exciting, inspirational, and help our productivity soar beyond our imaginations. Charles Dickens, Pablo Picasso, Mozart and Beethoven did not let anyone dictate their schedules. Their routines set them up to so they could properly work on their passions, and eventually reach success.

Routines don't only provide structure and order to our day, but when we personalize them, they allow us to tap into our inner self and extract the magic which can sometimes hide deep inside. Routines help us create an environment that engages the right elements at the right times so everything we need to achieve our dreams is available to us exactly when we need it.

Let's start with the old proverbs *"the early bird catches the worm"*, or *"early to bed early to rise"*.

Open your notebook. Write down the answer to this question. *Are you an early bird, or a night owl*? My answer to this question probably saved my life and my businesses.

Circadian Rhythms
A circadian rhythm is essentially the built-in 24-Hour clock your body runs on. Some argue that while these clocks are native to us, they are manipulated by our environment, such as light and dark. Many experts argue the reason we have so many sleep issues is because we aren't going to bed when the sun falls, and rising along with the sun (which coincidentally is awfully close to what society expects of us).

I believe our circadian rhythm is built in, and unique to each one of us. I think the sleep disorders we face are not because we are not following the cycle of light, but because we are going against our own internal clocks by following societal rules on how our day should be spent.

I went against my Circadian Rhythm for most of my life. This abuse led to several years of insomnia. I would be lucky to get two hours of sleep each night, and as you can imagine, this lack of sleep took it's toll.

I was irritable most of the time. It took an extraordinary amount of effort to concentrate and focus because my brain was not firing on all cylinders. I was missing opportunities because in order to function I had to be tunnel visioned. I was not performing at top shelf quality.

All this because I followed the rules on when I should go to bed.

As we discussed earlier, sleep is essential to health, so when I say following my unique circadian rhythm saved my life, that was no dramatic exaggeration.

Your unique circadian rhythm is the foundation for your routines. If you are not aligned with your body clock, your routines won't be either. This is why I asked you to write down in your notebook if you are an early bird or a night owl.

"I never could have done what I have done without the habits of punctuality, order, and diligence, without the determination to concentrate myself on one subject at a time."
- Charles Dickens

As we move through the rest of this chapter, I will share my routines, and those of some successful people. These examples are intended as a guide only, to put you on the right path, and to experiment with, but not to copy.

The A.M. Routine
9:00AM to Around 10:30AM

I am a night owl, and not a morning person. I'm not the type to jump out of bed and be ready for the day. I need to ease into things.

I start each day with an hour or so of studying while I drink my bulletproof coffee.

My coffee acts as my breakfast. It has a healthy helping of coconut oil and butter – healthy fats that not only feed my body, but my brain as well. Again, this is important because I am not so sharp in the morning.

Studying is a lot like exercise for me. I never want to do it, but I'm honestly happy I did once I am done. While I let my coffee work it's magic, I spend some time reading a non-fiction book (usually around business or marketing), or a collection of blog posts. I also spend time with video tutorials on YouTube. It all depends on the subject I want to learn about at the time.

The variety of subject matter keeps this routine from getting boring. In fact, by the time I am done, I'm pretty pumped up and ready for world domination.

There are those who say checking your email first thing is not a good way to start the day. While I tend to agree, having email nag you while you are trying to do other things certainly isn't wise either. Having peace of mind knowing there is nothing pressing in your inbox or calendar can help set the tone for the day. Unless I am working on a time sensitive project, email waits until after coffee and study time.

How Famous Creative People Used This Time (6-3)
Ben Franklin used this time for creative work. So did Ludwig Von Beethoven. Sigmend Freud was at his day job, as was Wolfgang Mozart. Richard Strauss used this time for exercise. Picasso slept.

How will you use this time?
Are you currently using this time to your advantage? What could you be doing instead that would be better?

Write the answer in your notebook.

The Early Evening Routine
4:30PM to Around 7:30PM

As entrepreneurs we underestimate the power of downtime. Contrary to what many experts say, working 18 hours a day is not the way to success. Exchanging work for a bit of fun and relaxation can go a long way towards being productive.

Fika
Around 4:30 each afternoon, I take a break from work and participate in the Swedish tradition known as Fika. My Fika takes many forms, but is typically tea or coffee, either on

the front porch or at our favorite cafe downtown.

I probably should not be telling you this, but on Friday's it is not uncommon for my wife and I to head over to one our favorite watering holes for some tapas and drinks.

The Great Outdoors
After Fika, my wife and I go for a good brisk walk. Sitting in front of a computer is not healthy (one of these days I'll move to a standing desk) so getting the blood flowing keeps everything working as it should.

It is not always easy in the harsh Idaho winters, but we simply wave when people drive by us giving us strange looks as we walk down the snow covered sidewalk in sub-freezing temperatures.

The Feast
My wife and I are avid eaters of real food. We cook everything from scratch, which takes some time. We have streamlined it a bit, but eating good food helps keep us fit and also feeds our brain. Dinner time is around 6:30PM.

How Famous Creative People Used This Time (6-3)
Ludwig Von Beethoven, Charles Dickens and Victor Hugo used this time for exercise, leisure and exercise. Mozart and Honore de Balzac split this time between leisure and creative work. Franz Kafka split the time between sleep and exercise.

How will you use this time?

Are you currently using this time to your advantage? What could you be doing instead that would be better?

Write the answer in your notebook.

No Sleep Til... Brooklyn
11:30PM to around 12:30PM or 1AM

One of the things that plagues entrepreneurs is sleep deprivation. Even if we do attempt to get a full nights rest in, it is hard to shut off our overactive minds. This is why I've adopted this third routine.

Every night at around 11:30 I stop working. I shut everything down, and turn my volume on my phone all the way down. My work day has officially come to an end, and I leave my office and head upstairs to the living room where I settle on the couch (often sharing it with my Red Tick Coon Hound named Bumpus) where I read a fiction book.

I was never much of a reader in the past, but I have found this activity is beneficial for me as it helps my brain switch gears from business to pleasure. My mind cannot focus on the day I am leaving behind, or the day ahead because it is too busy playing the movie my mind's eye creates as I read the story. As my mind relaxes, so does my body and before you know it, I am ready for my nightly meeting with Mr. Sandman.

How Famous Creative People Used This Time (6-3)
Many famous creatives use this time for sleep (Voltaire, Ben Franklin, Kurt Vonnegut, Beethoven), while Charles

Darwin, Freud, Kafka and Gustave Flaubert were letting their creative juices flow. Dickens, Thomas Mann and Kingsley Amis kicked back with a snack.

How will you use this time?
Are you currently using this time to your advantage? What could you be doing instead that would be better?

Write the answer in your notebook.

Find Your Own Routine
These three routines have made a huge difference in my productivity, and in my business. To keep them from getting stale, I switch things up with different fiction books, different pubs and cafes and different study topics. I also change the area where I walk, so the scenery doesn't get boring.

I also want to make it clear my day is not as rigid as I may have made it appear. There certainly is room for spontaneity. The ability to be flexible is paramount to both personal and business life.

Each one of us is different and it is important to settle into routines which play to our strengths and weaknesses. I have shown examples of how I and successful creative people use routines to maximize our productivity. As you can see, there is no formula, or "best practice" for setting a routine.

Throughout this chapter I asked you to think about how you could use the various times of day. Now it's time to grab your notebook and begin the process of creating your own routines. Use your answers above to shape your routine.

Start with a typical day
Make a list of all the things you need to get done in the day, and what times are optimal for you to work on those things.

Use these times to create a series of routines which allow you to be at your best at each critical point in the day.

Experiment
It will take some time to find the sweet spot. Do not be afraid to keep adjusting until you get it dialed in, but remember to give it time to work. Each change requires an adjustment period. You won't fall into it overnight.

SEVEN

Quit Stalling, Go Make It Happen

It's time to defy the lizard brain. One of the things I have not mentioned yet is the theory of perfection.

We have all been there. We want to make sure everything is just right. We plan, and that little voice tells us we're not ready, and that is the moment when the never ending planning cycle begins.
Planning your strategy is key, but there is a point where it becomes paralyzing. Knowing when to make the transition from the planning stage to the execution stage is tricky, especially when you have that little voice messing with you. So, lets take everything from the last couple of chapters and put it to work. By the end of this chapter, you will have executed on something important that has been sitting on a virtual shelf somewhere collecting dust.

Ready? Too bad, let's do this!

Tell That Little Voice To Bug Off
That little thing some call the lizard brain is a powerful thing. It steers you wrong more than it steers you right, so find a way to shut it off. Trust your gut, it's usually right and some call it the second heart.

Exercise, meditation, talking with people you trust and avoiding negative events and people are great ways to stifle the lizard brain. You also do not want to underestimate the power of food. The lizard brain feeds on sugar, so it is best to avoid sugars (especially processed/table sugars). If you want your gut to steer you right, you need to keep it healthy.

Now that you have the lizard brain at bay, grab your notebook.

Write down one thing that you need to get done but have been procrastinating. Got it? Good. Now, under that, write down why it's not done yet. Be honest, there is no judging here.

Now, use the work flow below to help guide you into completing this project and setting it loose into the wild.

Create A Deadline
You do not want to skimp on the planning, but you need to set deadlines to keep you on track. Live and die by these deadlines as they'll force you to move forward.

Write down the following in your notebook:

I will complete this project by [date].

Stop Trying To Make Your Plan Perfect
Your plan does not need to be perfect. You do the best you can, and "perfect" it as you get feedback from your

customers. Yes, you are going to make mistakes, and that is perfectly OK. We all have, and we'll all make more. But you know what? We all live to fight another day, and we'll also be a lot smarter than we were yesterday.

You already wrote down why you have not finished this project yet. Add anything else that prohibits it from being set free.

Execute

You have got your list of fixes and/or completions, and you have got a deadline. The only thing left is for you to act and make it happen. I know this seems simple – crazy simple. That's because it is. Our mind gets in the way, and makes things more complicated, which brings me to one more little thing...

The Entrepreneur Jitters

If you find yourself tweaking little things, and questioning decisions you have already made, it is what I call the entrepreneur jitters. It's your little voice trying to scare the hell out of you.

Fear is a powerful emotion. Fear of failure, and even fear of success. You mind plays the "What If" game, and it is important to remind yourself every single entrepreneur has been there at one point or another. It is as if it's some sort of initiation into entrepreneurship.

Trust your gut, and trust your plan (you know, the one you and I just now created).

Part Four
Getting Shit Done

"Well done is better than well said."
-Benjamin Franklin

EIGHT

Busy Versus Productive

The Pareto Principle says twenty percent of our efforts result in eighty percent of our forward motion.

You have heard it before. It goes by many names, but we all know it. We do, deep inside we know there's a lot of crap we do every day (like eMail) that actually does not move us forward, yet we keep doing it. Why?

Why We Choose Busy Instead Of Productivity

Well, there's a lot of reasons. First, knuckleheads keep telling us we need to be busy. If we aren't doing something every second of the day, we are not working hard enough – we are slackasses and are doomed to fail.

Another reason is fear. Fear of success. Fear of failure. We'll talk about failure later, but fear of success is something we rarely think or talk about, yet it's profoundly real.

Fear of success comes from being afraid of what others might think or say when you stand out. It's not that we fear the actual success, we fear having to deal with the jealousy, criticism and judgment from those around us – the people who love us.

Generally speaking, people do not want us to succeed because that means they have to be successful also (to be our "equal"), and they do not want to do that. This is why so many of us entrepreneurs hear things like "you're crazy" or "It'll never work". This is why it's critical to surround yourself with people who genuinely want you to succeed, and give you objective advice.

Another part of this is living the status quo is easy and comforting. You know what to expect and for some, as long as things are "OK", then why change? We get all nice and cozy in our comfort zone.

And then there's the thing that comes after success. If this book becomes wildly popular, there's huge pressure for my next book to be equally awesome if not more so.

It's not that we entrepreneurs do not intend to maintain our success, but the added pressure gives life to the voice of self doubt.

The Difference Between Busy and Productive

Remember back in school when the teacher sent you home with a bunch of worksheets to finish? You spent hours answering questions, solving math problems and analyzing what some author meant by a certain passage in a book.

That's busy work.

That crap never did anybody any good. All it did was give you a sense of learning, but it didn't actually translate knowledge into practical information you can apply to life. It proved you could copy something from a book onto a worksheet. It is even worse these days as the purpose is not to teach but instead to have kids pass a number of standardized tests. We have brought that learned behavior over to our business.

We're *following* task lists, checklists for this and that instead of actually executing our ideas. We are completing a math worksheet instead of balancing the checkbook. We're filling our day with useless shit because that is what school has taught us to do.

Examples of busy: email, over-learning, reading blogs, spending more time than needed on social networks, creating content, doing tasks which don't require you (editing video, seoing your site).

We feel productive when we scratch off everything on our list, but the devil is in the details. What's on the list? Are those items truly moving you forward – helping you create something – or are those items simply keeping you busy? It is not as simple as just getting things done, it's getting the things done that inch you forward to your Destination.

Here's how Dictionary.com defines Productivity:
(1) producing or having the power to produce; fertile
(2) yielding favorable or effective results
(3) economics

      a. producing or capable of producing goods and services that have monetary or exchange value: productive assets
      b. of or relating to such production: the productive processes of an industry
(4) resulting in: productive of good results

To be productive, lets spend some time with the Pareto Principle I mentioned earlier.
Each task you perform which falls outside of the scope of what your business does is time not well invested.

The first couple of chapters in this book helped you discover and create a business around your passion. This is where your focus should be. Your business is the most effective, and you will be the most happiest, when you focus on your passion and what you are good at.

Go back and re-read those last two paragraphs.

Eighty percent of what you are doing is likely not doing anything for your business and is making you unhappy. This double whammy is it's also preventing your business from achieving greatness, and it is preventing you from reaching your Destination.

Grab your notebook.

Write down the tasks you personally do each day. I know each day may be different, but capture everything you do for the business down. The idea is to get a birds eye view of what you do for the company.

You know the line in *Office Space*, when "the Bobs" ask Smykowsky, "*What would you say you do here?*". Yeah, if you could just go ahead and answer this question, that would be great, mmkay.

Sometimes things evolve in a way that doesn't make sense. In the movie, "the Bobs" identified what Smykowsky did could have been done differently. In fact, poor Smykowsky's entire position was eliminated because having a person to shuffle paperwork did not make sense. How this position came to be is anybody's guess, and while this is a fictional situation, I bet there are things on your list which will get you to say, "why am I doing this?".

Once you have your list, identify the 20% that accomplishes the following:

Tasks which move your company forward.
These tasks make your business run smoother, develops a company culture that inspires your team to do their best, and most importantly solves the tension and pain points of your customer.

Tasks which move you closer to your Destination
These tasks help YOU run smoother, and make you happy. These are things that make you happy to get out of bed each morning and head into the office. These are things YOU personally love to do, and are best suited to perform.

Assess each item, and if it doesn't fall into either category above, then move it to a separate page containing the 80% tasks.

Spend Some Time With The 80%
What is in the 80%? Take some time and segment these tasks into two areas;

Tasks that can be delegated.
These are tasks which can be delegated to a team member or outsourced.

Tasks that can be deleted.
These are tasks which do absolutely nothing for your business and should be removed.

My good friend, Ken Manesse Sr., says; "Systems run your business. People run your systems." Systems are a vital part of business, yet many of us fail to put the proper systems and people in place. So now we're armed with the 20% that will move our business forward, let's create the team to help us do exactly that.

NINE

You Can't Do It Alone

Creating The Team

Now that you have identified the tasks critical to the company's success, it is time to build a team around those tasks. There are several ways to approach this, but please understand this is something that absolutely must happen to ensure the success of your business.

Why is this so critical? Because **You Can't Do It Alone**. Believe me, I've tried.

Bootstrapping is the popular choice for many entrepreneurs. I love the idea of bootstrapping, but there's a dark side. Limited funds help us be creative with our solutions, but it also creates a certain mentality when it comes to where we choose to invest in our business.

I have always bootstrapped my businesses, and like many entrepreneurs I didn't want to invest in things I could do myself. I did not understand that it is not about paying for skills per se, it's about investing in time. The old adage "Time Is Money" is very true, and that is very easy to overlook

When you wear all of the hats, it's not possible to grow your business because you are spending all your time doing everything. You're barely keeping up with what has to be done. Even if you could get more customers, you would not have the time to service them properly.

What this means is by trying to do it all, even if you have the skill set to do it, limits what you and your company can achieve. There are only so many hours in the day, and you can only work so many of them. The more people you have on your team, the more hours of work can be achieved in a day.

So, I say again – You cannot do it alone, and you must have the right people for the right job. I know this sounds obvious, but what this actually means is creating a team passionate about what they do. The kind of passion that means they know what they're doing and they absolutely jump out of bed every morning to do it!

You want an accountant that is passionate about what finances mean to a business, and is willing to go beyond simply doing the books. You want customer service reps that rise to the challenge of satisfying even the most obnoxious customer. You want an IT guy that giggles like a schoolgirl when a new version of Linux is released (and obviously knows to make sure you've turned it off and on again).

As I mentioned earlier, you can build your team a number of ways. We don't live in a world of employee – employer relationships anymore. There are many other dynamics you can explore when putting together your all-star team.

Partnerships

Surprised to see this here? Partnerships are a great way to add expertise to a company, especially one that is new or struggling. A partner can offer a new set of eyes, add name recognition (especially if they have a strong audience/reputation), and depending on the arrangement, may offer a financial investment.

Collaboration

Some may think this isn't for everyone, but I disagree. I believe collaborating is the future of business. The idea of "mine" is slowly disintegrating in favor of mutually beneficial arrangements which often involve, are you ready for this – working with your competitors.

Collaboration is one of my favorite parts of business. I get to be creative, and tap into the knowledge and creativity of others whom in a traditional sense I would never get to work with. It's the most fun when two seemingly different industries get together to create something extraordinary, like a metal band performing with symphonies or at a ballet.

A desk manufacturer could collaborate with a health expert to create a standing desk that offers every health advantage. A greenhouse could partner with an ink manufacturer to create a non-toxic ink made from plants and flowers. A software programmer, an appliance manufacturer and a grocery store could collaborate on a refrigerator that automatically keeps itself stocked with everything you love. The possibilities are endless.

Virtual Assistants, or VAs
I know many "solopreneurs" who actually aren't solopreneurs at all. They build a team that includes one or more virtual assistants who take on tasks like screening and answering email, writing copy, product launches and other tasks critical to the business, but isn't something they themselves need (or want) to do.

VAs usually have built systems of their own that allow them to perform the task at hand quickly and easily. By hiring a VA, you tap into their system (we'll talk about systems in the next chapter).

Grab your notebook.

First, take some time to think about the culture of your company. By that I don't mean having a "jeans and Hawaiian shirt day", but if you want your team to be all in house (employees), virtual assistants, and if you are willing to bring a partner into the mix and give up a percentage of your company.

Having employees isn't as simple as hiring somebody. There are legal requirements which must be met (records that must be kept, taxes, healthcare, hour restrictions), training, providing equipment, payroll and other things that need to be considered when thinking about hiring employees.

No matter which route you decide, the objective is to create the best possible team that fits the company like a glove. There is no standard, right or wrong. Remember, you get to write the rules here, so create a culture that is in the best interest of the company AND the team.

Once you have that, let's dive into the actual tasks.

In the "delegated" part of your 20% list (which you created in chapter eight), break the many moving pieces up into the various categories (accounts, product development, marketing, sales).

For each of these categories and positions/tasks, ask the following questions:

Will these tasks require more than one person?
Will these tasks be best suited for a partner, a virtual assistant, an employee or company/firm?
Who do I know that can fill these positions?
Who do I know that knows someone who can fill these positions?

These questions should help in the right direction to find passionate people who will help you live your passion (while living theirs as well) while filling the positions the way your culture dictates.

Now that you have your all-star team, lets focus on the other end; systems.

TEN

How The Hell Do I Do That Again?

"Systems run your business, people run your systems". We covered the people part, now lets talk about the system part. These two things go hand in hand. You can't have one without the other.

Without systems, you do not have a business that can survive hardship. Nobody wants to think about these things, but what would happen to your family if you could not work at your business? If you're the only one who knows how to run the various moving parts of the business, it's likely your business would not survive, and your family would suffer.

Systems offer many benefits:
(1) Allow anyone to run the business as you would (making it possible to have that lifestyle business everybody keeps talking about).
(2) Allow your business the ability to be sold
(3) Make training easy and consistent
(4) Provides a consistent experience for your customers
(5) Makes your business scalable

What Is A System?

Systems are nothing more than a document (which may include audio and video) that outline the process of any given task in your business; answering the phones, paying vendors, shipping a widget, getting a store ready to open each morning) and the tools needed to complete these procedures.

Anything you or a team member does that you will do again, needs to be documented. Yes, this is an exceedingly tedious process, but by investing in building your systems, you will ensure your business has the mechanisms to survive without you, which ultimately translates to money.

There are two types of systems that can operate your business. The first are systems unique to your business that will be done by you or an in-house team member. These are systems you create.

The second are systems that are critical, but not unique, to your business. These are systems that can be outsourced (either through a firm or virtual assistant).

Outsourcing Your Systems

This can be a difficult thing for an entrepreneur. Giving up control and handing off critical parts to our business to someone else is scary. This way of thinking gets many entrepreneurs in trouble (including myself for a number of years).

As we talked about in the last chapter, you can hire virtual assistants to help you with tasks that aren't specific to your business (like transcriptions, editing, taxes). You are not only hiring their expertise, but you are also are paying for access to their system.

Hiring virtual assistants is not the only route. You can hire an entire company to handle a particular part of your business. I do this with my book distribution, as I illustrate a little later.

Creating Your Systems

I'm a fan of the simple. Creating a system is simple (but not easy). Below are the three steps I use to build my systems.

(1) Next time you do something you're going to do again (and again, and again), get a piece of paper and write down each step. Be extraordinarily detailed and specific. Include any tools/software programs needed to complete the task. Take screen shots, pictures and video to fully illustrate the process if necessary.

Remember the exercise you did in school where you had to explain something we all do and take for granted, like opening a door? Creating your system is exactly like that. Do not assume someone will know how to do something. If it needs to be done, put it down and detail how it should be done.

(2) Give this document to someone who has never done this task before, and ask them to follow your instructions.

Make notes on any parts which are confusing or unclear.

(3) Make the necessary tweaks to the document based on the feedback from Step 2, and repeat until the task can be done with the proper result solely by following the instructions in the document. Test this with several people to make sure the result is consistent and desirable.

Just because it's always done that way, doesn't mean that's the way it should be done.
One of the benefits that comes out of the system creation process is you often identify problems with your work flow, or discover ways you can do it better. As you create your system, keep an open mind and take it slow so you can see flaws and opportunities.

In Practice, Systems in The Real World.

This book you are reading right now utilized two different systems, which allows my business to earn money without me. Obviously I need to write the book (I don't believe in ghostwriting, but that would be an example of outsourcing a system), but once the initial work is done, my part in the process is finished.

System One: Book Formatting
Once I made the decision to self publish, I had to figure out how to convert my manuscript to the many formats needed for it to be sold and distributed.

I created a process involving the conversion of my

manuscript to PDF, then to e-reader (Nook, Kindle) and print formats. The system involves several steps and three programs.

System Two: Distribution
Once the book is formatted, it gets uploaded to my chosen distributors (Amazon, Barnes & Noble and Kobo) where their systems take over. Those distributors know the best way to distribute both my physical and digital books because that's what they do. They have the systems in place to take my book from my computer to the world.

A bonus to utilizing their system is I also get the benefit of their marketing efforts. Amazon gets more traffic than my site (which is targeted), and by tapping into their internal search engine, I sell more books than if I sold from my website alone (proving you can get more accomplished and reach a higher level of success if you get help).

Part V
Moving The Needle

"Always be yourself, express yourself, have faith in yourself, do not go out and look for a successful personality and duplicate it."
-Bruce Lee

ELEVEN

Failing Failure Who Fails

Failure: to fall short of success or achievement in something expected, attempted, desired, or approved

Let's tackle the failure thing. We are told failure is not an option. Failure is bad. It also comes in the form of a noun if you mess up – you're a failure. A lousy failure who fails. #fail.

You hear all sorts of experts and self help guru's saying failure isn't a bad thing. I have even heard some say we should strive for failure. No, we should not. Failure is a bad thing. In every single one of the definitions I found, none was positive.

I understand why the gurus want to turn failing into something positive. Our brains are full enough with self doubt that when failure hits, it could mean the end. However, thinking about failure in a positive context leads to a pattern of continuous failure because we are not acknowledging failing is something negative and something we should try to avoid.

Instead of trying to make failing something positive, let's stop focusing on the meaning of the word, and redirect our energy to our reaction to our failures.

Failing means we screwed up.

Let's cut the bullshit. Failing is not a good thing no matter how you slice it. You can try to redefine it based on a quote from Thomas Edison, but the reality is we cannot go changing the meaning of words to make ourselves feel better.

Failing means we made a mistake somewhere along the way. That failure needs to be acknowledged for what it is, and dealt with appropriately. Is it a bad thing? Yes, it is, but it's not the end of the world, nor is it the end of your business. The quote from Edison I eluded to earlier goes something like this:

> *"I have not failed 1,000 times. I have successfully discovered 1,000 ways to NOT make a light bulb."*

There are many versions of this quote out there, but they all basically say the same thing. Many took this quote to mean failing isn't a negative thing after all, but I see a different meaning.

I do not see Mr. Edison trying to change the meaning of failure to mean something positive, I see a man who reacted to his failures in a positive way.

Failure will sneak up behind you, shadow you, get to learn how you behave, and then out of nowhere it will strike, leaving you sticky, broke and confused

Here's the thing, while you should make every effort to avoid failure, no matter what you do, no matter how much you plan, no matter how much time you put in, no matter how far you think it through, failure is inevitable. It's unavoidable.

Because failure is inevitable, it's important to learn how to deal with it. How we react to failing determines whether we reach our Destination, or enter the perpetual cycle of failure.

As I mentioned above, the reason gurus try to redefine failure is so we don't let our self doubt take over and stop us from continuing. It's important for us to keep going, and in order to do that, we need to have the mechanisms in place to deal with failure in a positive way. We are not trying to make the failure positive, we're making our reaction to it something positive.

This distinction may seem small, but it changes the entire approach to moving past the failure itself. It is about getting in the right mindset which allows us to see what we need to see in order to move past the failure.

What went wrong?

It is not enough to simply try something new, or rethink the problem. It's important to understand why things failed in the first place. This is why I stress the importance of looking at failure as something bad. We have to acknowledge the bad, understand the why, so we can make moves to *correct* it so we don't continue to make the same mistakes which led to the failure.

Is the failure a result of something simple like the color of the button for your call to action, or is it something fundamental like not fully understanding the needs of your audience?

Answering these questions involves a process involving the retracing of our steps until we find the point where things drifted off course. It is not unlike the search for our lost keys, however it can be tricky because it's not always clear where the point of failure is, or even where things began to drift off course.

Several years ago I created a music company with the mission of creating a music industry which didn't involve record labels or other middlemen. The mission seemed simple, yet as I got deeper into this business, I began to see complexities that explained why bits and pieces were failing.

Musicians do not think of themselves as a business, nor do they want to. This is why record labels continue to exist, and artists strive to sign with them even though they offer no real value (and often times send the artists into bankruptcy).

The other complexity was the behavior of music fans. Apple, Pandora, and Spotify combined with the endless lawsuits by copyright lawyers changed the way fans experienced music. Music, while still very much important, because something fans expected to get free, in singles, or in inexpensive streaming. It was a very (and still is) a volatile time.

These were fundamental problems that required a total rethink of the business model. Had I continued to force my ideas, the company clearly would have failed. By identifying the key issues I faced, I was able to create a music company that served the artists the way they wanted to be served.

I had to get real honest with myself. Our natural instinct is to protect our ideas. They are our babies, and we want to see them grow up and live long healthy lives. We have to be realistic and know when it's time to make the changes we need in order to facilitate their long life.

In the case of my music company, it meant shuttering it and creating an entirely new company with different objectives and missions. Missions that align better with the needs of artists and their fans.

Finding the point of failure often requires a fresh pair of eyes – objective and experienced eyes. You cannot be afraid to ask for help when you need it. It's not actually about knowledge per se, it's about our perceptions.

If you missed it the first time, it is likely you will miss it again, even with the benefit of hindsight, not because you don't have the knowledge or the skill, but because it's extremely difficult to see every angle, especially through a protective lens.

Our need to protect those ideas often cloud our view, which means the truth is not always right there in front of us. Having fresh eyes can make the difference between continued failure and a course correction leading to your Destination.

For me, those eyes came in the form of artists and an extensive amount of research. I had numerous deep conversations with independent artists to completely understand their needs. I also had the same conversations with music fans because they are a vital piece of the puzzle. From this, I could now build the business around bridging the gap between the artist and the fan.

Talk to your Customers
I hear this advice all the time, but what about those entrepreneurs who don't have customers? Before I address this, I want to dispel a common myth floating around in the business community.

If you don't have customers, you don't have a business, you have a hobby.

Put that bullshit out of your head right now because it's not true. Every business begins at zero. Customers don't simply drop into your lap, you have to earn them. To get qualified customers, you need to have a business. The business comes first, then the customers come after you ramp things up to the point where you have proved your customer-worthy.

If you don't have customers yet, you most likely have an audience. Start building a relationship with them. Once you build a rapport with them, you can ask them the things you would ask a customer. Money does not have to be exchanged for feedback to be useful.

I would also recommend finding a mentor, or hiring a consultant to help you discover and fix your fail points. They have the experience and the objectivity to help you through the dark times of failure.

It is through failure we learn and grow. Success is not born, it's created slowly using one brick of failure at a time. How we handle our failures, both big and small, is the determining factor on not only if we reach success, but the speed in which we attain it.

Grab your notebook.

Identify a present or past failure. Write it down in your notebook. Make it tangible.

Think about your reaction to that failure, and if it's a past failure, how did you correct it? Were you able to correct it? Genuinely able to correct it, not sweep it under the rug?

In your notebook, take your failure (past or present) and write down the fail point, and how that fail point can be corrected.

I know what you're thinking. What's the point in working on a past failure? That particular failure could still be causing you problems today. There could be a pattern of behavior that leads up to failure, and this process can help identify it. By solving a past failure, you might avoid a failure lurking around the corner.

One more chapter to go, and it's about the holy grail.

TWELVE

Are You Successful? Would You Know It If You Were?

Success is like art. It means different things to different people. Some think success is defined by how much money accumulates in a bank account. Some think it's about how many followers you have racked up on social networks, or how high your Klout score is, or the amount of hits on your website.

Some think it is about having a large email list, or having a client roster that includes a few big names. Some believe success is appearing on Oprah, or some other television show "reaching millions of viewers".

Even dictionaries have trouble defining it. Dictionary.com has not one, but five different definitions:

(1) the favorable or prosperous termination of attempts or endeavors; the accomplishment of one's goals.
(2) The attainment of wealth, position, honors, or the like.
(3) A performance or achievement that is marked by success, as by the attainment of honors: *The play was an instant success.*

(4) A person or thing that has had success, as measured by attainment of goals, wealth, etc.: *She was great success on the talk show.*
(5) Obsolete, outcome

Grab your notebook. Turn to a fresh page and write down the answer to the following question. Don't over think it, simply write down what you believe to be success. No one is judging you, so let the answer flow through you and onto the paper.

"***When will I consider myself successful?***"

Societal Influence

All of those measures of success I mentioned earlier is society's influence dictating what we should think and strive for. *No matter if you're an employee or an entrepreneur, success is the same and has been clearly defined for you.*

The way we think about success created an unnatural and unhealthy aversion to failure. We look at success and failure as polar opposites, but as we just now talked about, failure (or your reaction to it) is how you reach success, not avoid it.

Society's idea of success is clearly a status and numbers game. It's about winning, not losing. It is about being right, and not being wrong. This line of thinking is what gets entrepreneurs into trouble.

Success Is The Root Of All Evil

OK, maybe not, but it certainly creates an environment for evil to manifest and thrive. There's a popular line often paraphrased from the bible which says "Money is the root of all evil." Since success is largely defined by how much money is in the coffers, it's not a stretch to say success is the root of all evil.

I do believe the sentiment of this verse to be incredibly powerful, and one too often ignored, as I'll demonstrate with a little stroll through the aisles of a typical grocery store.

As you go up and down each aisle, consider the company names on the boxes as they sit comfortably on the store shelves.

One could clearly argue these companies are successful. They are multinational companies making billions of dollars in revenue each quarter. Everyone knows their names, and it's not uncommon for these products to sell out during sales.

But there's a dark side.

Let's take a look inside our virtual shopping cart full of well known brands. What do you see? If you look closely, you will see a collection of ingredients that are not designed to provide you with healthy sustenance, but to provide you with something that tastes good while using the cheapest ingredients possible under the law (which is pretty liberal).

Is it a coincidence that as our food has become more processed, and under the control of a handful of companies, we are now seeing an increasing number of health issues – heart disease and Type II Diabetes to name just two?

The point here is not to debate the correlation of processed food and poor health, but to illustrate when we use money to guide us in business, we no longer operate in the best interest of those we went into business to serve.

Derek Sivers, the man behind CD Baby, says you should

set up your business like you don't need the money. CD Baby started as a way for Derek to sell his own music online. It was never intended as a business, yet as more and more people wanted his solution, it grew to serve thousands of musicians all over the world, and eventually sold for several million dollars.

Derek ran his business to reach his own successes. It was less about the money, and more about making people happy. Putting a smile on everyone's face who made the decision to work with him.

He often tells the story of his solution to a problem many entrepreneurs face – the client who wants change after change. His solution was not to charge them more, or even say no to more changes (leaving the customer unsatisfied), but to say, that if a change was needed, all that was required was a pizza.

Yes, a pizza. Who doesn't love pizza? Win-Win.

By tapping into his idea of success, CD Baby became successful by any definition, but most importantly, it became successful by Derek's standards.

Don't get me wrong, I don't hate money. It's necessary in the world we live in, and the financial side of your business isn't something to be ignored. The point here is, do not let money be your guide.

Pride (In The Name Of Love)

If money is one of the deadly sins in business, then we have to talk about pride.

In business, pride manifests itself in many ways, but one of the most accepted, and often encouraged, is follower counts and "scores of influence". We track things like how many shares our posts have, or how many hits our website receives daily.

We create demagogues (whom we call "influencers") and follow everything they say, because we want to be exactly like them someday.

While money is at least important because it is how we pay our bills and put food on the table, focusing on the elements of social pride serve zero purpose in creating a stable business. Sure, one could argue others are also looking at these things to judge you and your competence, so lets take a slight psychological detour.

There are many factors of influence, one of which is what we are talking about here; social proof.

According to Dr. Robert Cialdini, social proof is one means we use to determine what is correct. When we are uncertain, we use the actions of others to decide how we should proceed forward. (12-1)

Cialdini also points out 95% of people are imitators, while

only 5% are the initiators. Now, when you start to add up everything, you begin to see those 5% are the influencers. They are the ones who are finding a niche and dominating it. (12-1)

What's fascinating is because these influencers – the 5% - are focused on providing solutions to problems, their social proof occurs naturally.

Iron Maiden's gonna get you, no matter how far.
One of my favorite bands is Iron Maiden. There's no doubt this metal band has reached legendary success, but where they are now is not important, it's how they got here.

Iron Maiden started out just like any other band, so why did they succeed when others did not?

They worked hard to build a loyal fan base. This took an extraordinary amount of patience, determination, and providing the best possible experience for the music fan who showed up to watch them perform.

This didn't happen overnight, in fact it took a few years of traveling (living) in a van to obtain these loyal fans, most of whom never heard of Iron Maiden before. These guys literally had no following.

Fast forward to one night five years in the making.

The story (12-2) goes, a label representative went to see them play for the purpose of signing them. He had to decide between Iron Maiden and Def Leppard. When he arrived, the club was so packed with fans, he couldn't get in.

Even when Iron Maiden started playing, he could barely hear them over the screaming fans who had packed the club to see their favorite band.

Even though the label representative could not see or hear the band, Iron Maiden was signed to EMI that night.

It was not the amount of people in the club, but the fact that the fans were so engaged with this band. They weren't simply standing there, but jumping, screaming and chanting. They had to see this band. It was not a request, it was a demand.

Let's not forget social proof is something earned, not simply gained. We can increase our follower counts many different ways, but the best way is to focus not on the numbers themselves, but the people behind the numbers. Iron Maiden of course wanted fans, because fans translated into money, but instead of focusing on counting the ticket sales at each venue where they performed, they focused on performing music that resonated with the fans.

They innovated their performance, created "Eddie", a monster who would spit blood over the drummer, and eventually became a larger than life size character who would terrorize the entire band on stage to the delight of the crowd.

Iron Maiden *took* pride from their work. The work came first, and the pride they received was a result of that work. Nearly 40 years later, Iron Maiden still packs stadiums and sells records, while those who focused on sales and "making it big" find themselves singing into a drive-thru microphone in front of a very different crowd.

The Rule Breaking Definition Of Success

To understand success, and how it's obtained and what exactly it is, I studied people like Richard Branson, Howard Schultz and Elon Musk, and reverse engineered their journey to discover the *secret of success*.

What I learned that while it is no secret, it is indeed hidden. We are taught to look to lists and formulas to point us in the direction of success. It's not about any of those things, success is about two things, which brings me to the definition.

Success is achieved when both the entrepreneur and their customer is unbelievably happy.

(1) Success is achieved when YOU, the entrepreneur, is unbelievably happy.
This is why living your passion as your foundation will lead you to success.

(2) Success is achieved when your customer is

unbelievably happy.
If your focus is making the customer happy, and not inflating your ego and bank account, the coveted word of mouth will grow exponentially, thus leading to success.

Grab your notebook.

In the beginning of this chapter I asked you to write down how you defined your success. Now, I want to ask the same question, framed a different way. Open your notebook, and write down the answer to the following question (as it relates to your business):

"*What Makes Me Happy?*"

Got it down? Good.

OK, think about how your first answer compares to what you just now wrote down. Write your thoughts down in your notebook to make them tangible.

Next, I want to backtrack a little to Chapter 2 when we talked about finding your passion. Your answer here, and what you wrote down for your passion should be the same thing, because if you are living your passion, happiness isn't too far away.

Epilogue
A Story To Tie It All Together

There's a certain romance that surrounds the entrepreneurial lifestyle. The idea of being your own boss, working when you want to, and doing what you love every single day and making money doing it sounds like a dream come true.

Being an entrepreneur isn't all puppy dogs and rainbows. To create your dream, you have to be willing to do the hard things to make shit happen.

Dreams Don't Realize Themselves

Last year around this time, I weighed nearly 100 pounds more than I do right now. Not only was I a fat ass, but my overall health was poor with chronic sinus infections, gout and insomnia. I was a bear to be around, and, well, let's just say things weren't pretty.

I love food, and I knew depriving myself of foods I love wasn't going to work. My wife and I had already been looking into the quality of our food and had made some changes, but it wasn't until we dove deep into the issue did we understand what it would take to realize the changes we sought. We needed to change the entire idea of how food relates to our body. It's not about enjoyment per se, it's about fuel. Our bodies depend on the nutrients we feed it, and once we understood that processed foods, sugar and wheat were doing harm to us, we figured out a way to rid them from our diet. These were things we relied heavily on to sustain us, and it was killing us.

It would have been easy to say, "I can't give up sugar", or "I can't give up bread". But you know what, when you want something bad enough, you make it happen. It's not going to happen on it's own.

Success Doesn't Come With An Easy Button

I dedicated myself to curing my ailments. I researched proper diet (not dieting, but diet) and experimented until I found the one my body responded to the best. It meant doing the following:

Growing most of our vegetables
I built a 700 square foot greenhouse in my backyard, which included a 250 gallon aquaponic system. I spent almost a year planning, and another couple of months doing the actual building. I quite literally built a system to grow food.

Cooking all our meals from scratch.
Cutting out the processed stuff means longer times in the kitchen preparing meals and cleaning up after them. There's also the added time of planning each meal. Creating systems helped streamline the tasks of cooking and cleaning, making it much easier and fun.

Fighting the cravings as my body detoxed

The body can be cruel as it detoxes, and staying on the path when things got rough wasn't very pretty sometimes.

Learning what caused the cravings, and avoiding those foods (while eating those foods that squashed cravings like dark chocolate) helped lease the fight.

Learning as much as possible about nutrition and health
There is a lot of misinformation out there about nutrition, much of it put out by seemingly trusted sources like doctors and governments. Finding reliable and trustworthy sources was time consuming and challenging.

Dealing with some uncomfortable social situations
The world revolves around processed foods (well in the US anyway). Finding ways to politely say no to something while not offending the host isn't an easy thing to accomplish, even when you explain why (people don't always understand).

It Doesn't Happen Overnight
This journey started over three years ago, and will continue because it's now part of who I am. It's only been the last eight months that I've started to see the result of all my hard work (and that of my wife).

It would have been easy to say "fuck it" when things started getting difficult, and the results weren't visible (although they were indeed there), but sticking with it and keeping my eye on the dream resulted in several things:

I'm much healthier
The sinus infections are gone, my gout attacks are much less frequent than before (and when they do occur, it's because I've deviated from my plan), and I now sleep like a baby. A third of my weight is gone, which means my clothes fit better, and I look better (which in a society that judges based on looks, improves my chances in business).

My mind is clear and focused
The fuzz that used to fill my head is now gone, allowing me to tap into parts of me I didn't know existed. Because of this, I've been able to achieve more in my business in the last three months, than I have in the last decade.

I've discovered what's legitimately important
I learned that I was focusing on things that were setting me up to fail. I was following, not breaking rules (leading). It was always inside me, but I wasn't able to let it out.

You Can't Do It Alone
Just because you may be a solopreneur doesn't mean you have to do it all. It's less about competition and more about collaboration.

I couldn't have transformed my health alone. My wife helped do the research (in fact she did most of it), people who have been doing this a lot longer than me were gracious enough to share their knowledge and kept me inspired to push forward every day. Even the ranchers who I buy my grass fed/pastured meat from- a partnership outlasting the meal bringing us together.

Whether we want to acknowledge them or not, we all have weaknesses which would benefit from someone else's strength. In addition, there are only so many things we can do on our own. Ideas become stronger and more robust when we bounce them off others.

Setting Yourself Up To Succeed
If building a successful business was about magical formulas, checklists and easy buttons, then we wouldn't have so many failed businesses.

Dreams are reached with determination, learning from many failures, and wanting that dream so much you are willing to do the hard stuff and actually earn your success. And the meal of success wouldn't be complete without a slice of patience for dessert.

Thank You!

I would like to thank you for purchasing my book. Really, I mean it. I know this book is a bit unconventional, but that's what coloring outside the lines is really about, right? If we are not breaking a few rules, then we must be following them. Who wants that?

I have one last thing to ask of you. This time it doesn't involve your notebook. I hope you enjoyed this book, and it would mean a lot to me if you could leave a review of this book on the site where you purchased it.

I don't really care about "Five-star" reviews, but I do care that I'm meeting the goals that I set out to do, and your honest review can help me do exactly that.

Thank you, and I wish you well as you travel on your journey to your Destination.

Toodles.

Special Thanks

Below are some people who have supported and influenced me over the last year or so.
I am truly grateful for your kindness, support and for sharing your wisdom and thoughts with me.

Kate Bowyer, Mike Svensson, Jessica Dewell, Nora Whalen, Ken Menasse Sr., Zara Altair, Todd Lebeauc, Frank Gainsford, Sheila Hensley and Stephanie Sims

Sources

(3-1) From Dictionary.com

(3-2) http://www.howtofascinate.com/products-and-pricing/fascination-advantage-report/

(6-1) *Food Rules, A Doctor's Guide To Healthy Eating*, Dr. Cate Shanahan, M.D.

(6-2) http://articles.mercola.com/sites/articles/archive/2013/01/21/sweetened-beverages-increase-depression-risk.aspx , Dr. Joseph Mercola, M.D.

(6-3) http://www.fastcodesign.com/3032874/infographic-of-the-day/the-daily-routines-of-26-of-historys-most-creative-minds

(12-1) *Influence. The Psychology Of Persuasion* by Robert Cialdini, PH. D.

(12-2) *The History of Iron Maiden – The Early Days*

www.ingramcontent.com/pod-product-compliance
Lightning Source LLC
Chambersburg PA
CBHW051733170526
45167CB00002B/915